Jesus On My Shoulder

The Life of A Police Officer

by Sgt. Dennis R. Sands

DORRANCE
PUBLISHING CO
EST. 1920
PITTSBURGH, PENNSYLVANIA 15238

The contents of this work, including, but not limited to, the accuracy of events, people, and places depicted; opinions expressed; permission to use previously published materials included; and any advice given or actions advocated are solely the responsibility of the author, who assumes all liability for said work and indemnifies the publisher against any claims stemming from publication of the work.

Dorrance Publishing Co
585 Alpha Drive
Suite 103
Pittsburgh, PA 15238
Visit our website at *www.dorrancebookstore.com*

ISBN: 979-8-89127-694-9
eISBN: 979-8-89127-192-0

Jesus On My Shoulder

The Life of A Police Officer

Contents

Introduction

I've walked the walk, so I can talk the talk.

This book is dedicated to all of the public supporters of law enforcement. These true events may be considered unbelievable, but they actually did happen. Every citizen, every police recruit, and every person considering a career in law enforcement should be exposed to the life of a police officer so they can answer the question "What would I do if . . . ?"

Each day as a police officer is different than any day before. If you are on the job, you must be mentally and physically ready for what comes next. It may be a day when you are bored. It may be a day of routine calls, such as traffic accidents or minor reports. But someday there will be a day that after what happened on your shift, you cannot go to sleep that night. I guarantee it.

The stories that you are about to read are true stories. Each one happened. All happened in DeKalb County, Illinois. Some of the stories may be hard to believe. A few are funny. A few are unbelievable. A few are downright nasty. But they are a story about the life of one police officer, Sergeant Dennis R. Sands.

Now, I am not a religious fanatic. I was baptized, confirmed into the Church, and married in a church, but throughout my adult life I rarely went to church.

Years after I retired, I woke up one night from a dream about some of my police encounters, which I often did. *Why?* I asked myself, half asleep. *Why could I get a dangerous call or find myself in a crucial or totally unexpected situation and always, and I mean always, have a sense of calmness and confidence that I can handle it?*

Reflecting back on my career in that moment, it suddenly dawned on me. Maybe, just maybe, there was a reason for *Why?* I had never thought this way before that night. Without my realizing it, I had had a helper on my shoulder all along in my career.

I woke up completely with an amazing story to tell! I had the answer to *Why?* Now, I also had a title for a book: *Jesus on My Shoulder*! Welcome to my story. I hope you find it entertaining, constructive, and inspirational.

My daughter, Becky, has been after me for years to write a book about the police stories I had told her, and now I have finally answered her request.

Please put yourself in my shoes. *What would you do if . . . ?*

Chapter 1

Machinegun Fire in a County Forest Preserve

It was a cool fall afternoon. Everything was quiet and peaceful. I was on patrol in my squad car, Zebra 12, and I decided to drive through the Sannauk Forest Preserve in southern DeKalb County to look at the fall foliage. Sometimes during hunting season, we got deer hunters who illegally chased deer out of the preserve into open fields. Often unarmed hunters would bang sticks against trees to illegally chase the deer out of the preserve. Then they could legally shoot them. So, I was on alert for any nearby gunfire.

As I drove around a curve in the road and down a small hill, I was shocked to hear automatic gunfire! I immediately stopped to figure out where the distant gunfire was coming from. I radioed dispatch about the gunfire and my location. The gunfire was coming from the east of me. There is a small creek that flows through that area.

I got out of my squad car. As I walked down the hill, I heard a second burst of gunfire. I recognized this as being from an automatic weapon like a machinegun. I updated dispatch, and they notified both the Somonauk and Sandwich police departments, each five to ten minutes away. They had backup coming. There were no county squad cars within thirty miles.

The creek at Sannauk Forest Preserve

I was able to jump from tree to tree, down to the creek area. Then another burst of machinegun fire! Peeking around the tree I had just jumped behind; I was able to zero in on the exact location. It was on a treelined hillside on the other side of the creek. I could see two people, a man and a woman, and a pickup truck. Both subjects appeared to be in their early twenties.

Seeing that they were on the other side of the creek, I backed up, hustling from tree to tree to my squad car. I notified the two city backup cars that gunfire was from the east side of the creek. We would have to approach the offenders from the east through the local airport property. They should meet me at the airport entrance.

I met with the Somonauk and Sandwich units and filled them in on what I saw and heard. They both said at the same time, "Now what?!" I had that sense of calmness. I knew what I needed to do. First, I needed to reduce their stress. I confidently described my thoughts and plan. They would back me up with loaded shotguns.

I joked with them about not shooting me. Nothing reduces tension quicker than a laugh. I could see both were now relieved and relaxed. They were confident in the plan and ready to execute it. We left our cars out of sight and got up to the tree line. We noticed there had been no more firings. As we moved singly from tree to tree, we could see their pickup truck.

One more factor to consider: There was a large dog panting in the truck bed. We could see the driver's door was open. There was a pair of legs extending out the doorway.

Obviously, the couple was preoccupied with each other. This was the big break we had hoped for. But how was the dog going to react? As I approached the truck, the two officers had their shotguns pointed and ready. The dog just looked at me with his tongue out and tail wagging.

I was able to walk right up, my gun drawn, to the open door and shout, "Police! Do not move until I tell you to move!" Both of their heads popped up, but they lay still. I sternly said, "I have two officers with me, and they have shotguns pointed at you."

I ordered the male to slide out first. One of the officers immediately handcuffed him. The other officer handcuffed the female as she slid out. The dog remained calm with his tongue out.

The male admitted the gun was his. I told him machineguns are illegal unless you have a special license. He said he knew that. He was just having some fun with his girlfriend, shooting tin cans.

I told him he was under arrest for possession of an illegal firearm and shooting it in a forest preserve. I transported him to the DeKalb County Jail. The gun was put into the evidence locker. I thanked the two officers and later personally talked to their chiefs of police about what a great job they did.

We all received commendations from our respective departments.

A few days later, I received a call from a federal agent. The male perpetrator was already on their radar as a major drug dealer in Chicago. They wanted my permission to bargain my charges for major drug information. He was willing to give them information about drug shipments between Texas and the Sandwich airport. Of course, I agreed!

I didn't realize it at the time, but I had a third partner on my shoulder guiding my every move.

Chapter 2

Suicide by a Nine-Year-Old Boy

Dispatch advised our south zone officer that the local fire department was reporting a death involving a young juvenile. As shift sergeant, I advised dispatch I would be on the way also. A short while later, dispatch informed me that all of the detectives were tied up and I should take over the investigation.

Upon my arrival, the paramedics were loading a nine-year-old child onto a stretcher. They were enroute to the local hospital. I asked the young deputy on scene what he had learned. He said the head wound was apparently self-inflicted. I asked where the weapon was, and he told me he had picked it up and put it in his car's trunk. A bad situation just turned worse.

A possible crime scene had been contaminated. I calmly explained to the deputy proper procedure. If possible, don't contaminate the scene until it is processed. I calmed him down, and after taking a few pictures we went to the hospital.

At the hospital, I interviewed the parents. We bonded because I also had a nine-year-old son at home. It was a tough conversation. Probably one of the toughest I had in my career. How I made it through, I didn't know. But I think I know now.

The dad explained that he had the gun in a box in one room and the ammunition in another part of the house, away from the gun. He said to his knowledge his son had never fired the gun before.

They told me their son had complained about being teased and bullied at school. I called the school and talked to his teacher. She verified that students had been picking on him. Her class was getting counseling both for the bullying and the student's death. The students involved confessed to teasing him about his dad's gun. They also teased him to fire it.

Now came the hardest part for me. I needed to take investigative pictures of the entrance wound and the exit wound of the child's head. The nurse helped me position the child as I took several photos of the entrance and exit wounds. All I could see was my own son lying there.

I went to my squad car and narrated my report. When I got home, I gave my son an extra hug! I didn't sleep much that night.

This is an example of what happens in policework. It becomes personal. As much as you try not to take it home with you, you will. I definitely had help getting through this tragedy.

Chapter 3

Close Acquaintance Threatening Suicide, Fires Gun at My Squad Car, Turns Hero!

This is a tough episode to write about because as a local police officer you will get serious calls about friends, relatives, and personal acquittances. This call involves an out-of-control man, serious gunfire, hilarious happenings, and a happy ending. Thank goodness I had that guy on my shoulder. This could have been tragic!

I was home on a lunch break when I got a call from the chief of police of next town to my east. A local man who I knew personally was drunk again and shouting obscenities at his neighbors. The chief and the man did not get along at all. The chief asked if I could go settle him down because I had done that before. When I arrived at his residence, I was met outside by the man's son.

The son told me his dad was on a three-day drinking binge and that he has a loaded pistol out. I cautiously walked up to the front porch and the man met me at door, the screen door locked shut. I asked him what was going on, and he said his wife had left him, his son was mad at him, and his mother had been berating him endlessly.

We talked for about five to ten minutes, greeting each other as old friends, asking about how the other was doing—anything to ease his mental attitude. I was there as much as a friend as a police officer. He unlocked the door and invited me to sit down. I sat in a chair, and he sat on a couch. As he sat down, I noticed a pillow slide forward, exposing his pistol. He immediately pushed the cushion back, but it was too late—I knew where the gun was now.

He showed me a tablet of yellow paper he had been scribbling all over. On it he had listed his pallbearers. The first name on the list was my own brother-in-law. He was slowly calming down and relaxing and crying. Then all hell broke loose as his mother came in through the back door and started berating him—calling him a loser, a drunk, and worthless person. I immediately got up and escorted her out of the house. I told the officers outside to keep an eye on her and that she was *not* to get back in the house.

About this time the sheriff, also a friend of the man, and the captain arrived on scene. I filled them in on what had taken place. The sheriff volunteered *me* to go back and make recontact with him. We could hear him yelling loudly, arguing on the phone with his wife. He was screaming into the phone, not making any sense.

Saving pine trees

As I began to walk back to the house, something made me pause by a row of pine trees to collect my thoughts for a few moments.

Suddenly the yelling stopped. Two shots were fired from inside the house through a bay window and struck my squad car twice. If I hadn't paused, I would have been in the direct line of fire. We all hit the ground behind cover.

Then he came charging out of the house down the porch steps. He had the gun down at his side, not pointing it at anyone. He noticed his friend, the sheriff, standing behind his squad car.

He challenged the sheriff to an old-fashioned gun duel in the middle of the street! He even offered to the sheriff that he could draw first. When the sheriff did not respond, the man turned around and walked back into the house.

A detective, another friend of the man, showed up at this time. We had a conference about how to proceed. The sheriff asked again if I would try and make contact with him. His front yard was a series of big trees. I moved from tree to tree, shouting out his name. As I advanced, the detective took my position as we advanced toward the front porch steps.

As we got to the steps, he was behind the locked screen door. He did not have the gun in either hand. We asked him to let us in. Soon the sheriff joined us on the steps. The door was still locked. The subject became agitated with us. He didn't like being told what to do.

He bent over and picked up the gun. All three of us reached for our guns, knocking each other off the steps. We must have looked like the Three Stooges. Very embarrassing!

The man thought it was very funny and after a few moments, he unlocked the door and let us in. We all walked into his living room, forming a triangle around him, with someone always on his back side.

We were ready to grab him if he raised the gun. He looked very tired and worn out from lack of sleep. We were waiting for the sheriff to nod his head, a signal to grab him. Suddenly, he tossed the gun to the sheriff. The detective and I immediately grabbed him.

Now comes the best part of the story! As we escorted the subject out through the kitchen door to the front porch, he suddenly broke loose. The three of us all grabbed at him as he pulled us through the kitchen door to the front porch. As we tried to secure him, we all fell down on the porch, right next to a bag of old rotten garbage full of maggots. He reached over and grabbed the garbage bag, and I knew instinctively to duck. The man dumped the garbage and maggots all over the sheriff! Once again somebody on my shoulder was helping me out of a mess.

He was handcuffed and put in a squad car to be transported to a mental hospital.

A few years later, there was a bank robbery in the northern part of DeKalb County. It just so happened our friend was walking past the bank as the bank robber was exiting. A bank employee was not far behind him, yelling, "Bank robbery!"

Genoa Bank

Our friend was right in the path of the escaping robber. He tackled the robber and held him until the police got there. For that he got a city commendation and his picture on the front page of the local newspaper! It was great to see he had turned his life around. He had a helper also!

Chapter 4

A Fishing Story!

Some of Jesus' first disciples were fishermen. I've got that in common with them. Sometimes it just helps to tell a good fish story.

We received a call about a domestic incident in which a male was walking around his backyard with a loaded gun. I drove my squad car down an alleyway. In the backyard was the male, an old dusty pickup truck, and a garage. As I approached, he walked to the other side of the truck and stopped.

I parked my car at an angle for protection. I was able to engage the man in a conversation. He refused to put the gun down and several times he put it against his temple or in his mouth. He did not threaten me in any way. However, I was extremely cautious of his movements. We talked for several minutes. To lighten the mood, I asked him if he liked to fish. He said, "Yes, I fish a lot."

We traded a couple of fish stories to lighten the mood. I was able to safely maneuver up to the old dusty truck. I drew an *X* on the dusty hood of the truck. I told him that when he was ready, he was to place the gun on the *X*.

Things were going well. I was making progress in calming him down. Then we were rudely interrupted. Our SWAT team was now on the scene, and they were getting anxious to get involved. They ordered me to give the man my telephone to talk to one of the SWAT negotiators. Against my better judgment, I handed him the phone. All the man did was laugh at her. I think he was mad at every woman that ever existed. The SWAT team was ruining my rapport.

I took my phone back and repeated my request for him to place the gun on the *X* on the dusty hood. Within a minute or two, he walked over to the truck and placed the gun on the *X*. I walked up to him; he turned around, and I handcuffed him. He was taken to the psych ward at the hospital. I went home and dreamed about fishing.

The next day, I was asked by the sheriff why I was not at the SWAT debriefing late the night before. After telling him the story about the SWAT team interrupting my negotiations against my wishes, he said, "Good job," and put me in for a citation. *He* was going to talk to the SWAT team.

Chapter 5

Domestic, Knife Wound across Chest

I received a domestic violence call at a local apartment complex in the county's jurisdiction. Upon arrival, I walked up to the building and noticed a man at the bottom of the stairs with no shirt on. As he turned toward me, I could see what appeared to a long knife wound stretching from his shoulder across his chest and down to his stomach. The wound seemed superficial. A little blood but not life-threatening.

I asked him, "Who did that to you?" He said his girlfriend. I asked, "Where is she?" He told me it was the second-floor west apartment as he pointed toward the door. I radioed dispatch for backup. The city responded with two cars. The city cars were there within a couple of minutes. They had been monitoring my status. Thank God the two departments had tremendous cooperation at the street level.

As I walked up the stairs and toward the apartment, the door opened. A young woman stood there holding a knife, screaming about her boyfriend. I ordered her to drop the knife, which she did right away. I kicked the knife behind the open door. She had bruises and scratches on her body.

There was a terrible odor of alcohol coming from inside the apartment, which looked like a warzone. Everything from pots and pans to ironing board and iron and several kinds of fruits and vegetables were scattered across the place. The furniture was turned over, and vomit was spilled all over the kitchen and living area.

After interviewing both parties, I decided to arrest both of them on domestic battery charges. Thank God the city police responded so quickly, keeping the couple separated while I talked to each of them. Both subjects were highly intoxicated, angry, and yelling—totally out of reality. Yes, I had help coming from two places: the city police and that guy on my shoulder.

Chapter 6

You're a Dog; You're Going to Bite Me!

I was cruising around one of our small towns one night when I saw a sixteen-year-old girl stumbling around an intersection. It was dark out, and she had dark clothing on. I shined the spotlight on her, and she started to run down the middle of the street. She kept saying, "You're a dog; you're going to bite me!"

Now at that time, I had been a police officer for years, and I never had anyone call me a dog. Lots of other names, but not a dog. She circled back toward the intersection. I could tell she was extremely high on drugs, probably LSD.

I radioed dispatch to send me an ambulance. I had a young juvenile hysterical on drugs. Shortly after that a car came down the road, with three juvenile boys in the car. They stopped but said they did not know her. Suddenly she ran to the boys' car and got in the back seat, still screaming about how I was going to bite her.

I told the driver to stay parked and that an ambulance was on the way. As long as I stayed back, the girl began to calm down. In a short while the ambulance showed up. After filling the paramedics in, we went to the car to get her on a stretcher. As you can imagine, she went nuts again, yelling and screaming. I was helping the paramedics get her out of the car when she twisted herself and kicked me full force in the back of my head!

Now *I* was seeing stars and out of it. I fell to the ground. The paramedics were successful in getting her on the stretcher. I was able to right myself and I explained to them I would be following them to the hospital. They asked if I was okay, and they gave me a sobriety-like test, which I passed. The life of a patrol officer is always at risk—no wonder we need divine help!

Chapter 7

Ring-Around the Squad Car (Kid with Knife)

I was in the same small town as the previous story, serving civil papers, which is another job of the sheriff's department. I heard two people screaming at each other from the yard next door. Then I noticed a man running from a fifteen-year-old juvenile who had a long knife. The juvenile was threatening to kill the man. I radioed for backup. Dispatch was sending the nearest car, which was ten to fifteen minutes away.

I immediately yelled at the kid to stop and drop the knife. The man, his stepdad, had made it to the front porch and got in the house. The juvenile turned all of his anger toward me. He ran over to my squad car nearby me. As he kept coming and threatening me, I used the squad car as an in-between. We began to play ring-around the squad car!

I tried to calm him down as we went one direction, then another, around the squad car. I did not want to shoot him, but I did have my gun out. I basically was stalling until backup got there.

Then, the improbable happened. A train was blocking the street my backups were on.

All of a sudden, the stepdad had inexplicably opened the front doorway, and the kid went running back toward the house. This was just the distraction I needed! The stepdad yelled at the kid and closed the door, just in time to block the knife the kid had just thrown at him.

At this point, I had approached the kid from behind, and I took the chance to tackle him. I handcuffed him, and then I saw my backup officer coming down the street. He helped me get the kid into my squad. I told the stepdad and mom I was taking the kid to the hospital psych ward and that they should meet me there.

To this day I've marveled at what possibly could have possessed the stepdad to reopen the door at the exact time I needed him to do that. Was someone whispering on *his* shoulder too?

Chapter 8

What a Way to Spend Easter Sunday!

One quiet Easter Sunday, we received a call to a local trailer park. A resident was reporting that his adult son, who also lived in the trailer park, was threatening suicide with a rifle.

We were given the lot number, and we had three cars responding. Upon arrival, I sent one deputy to talk to the dad and one deputy three trailers south of the man's trailer. I positioned myself three trailers east of the man's trailer, which was in the far north row of trailers in the park.

The dad was on the phone with dispatch. As soon as the deputy entered the dad's trailer, the dad hung up with dispatch. He then called his son and started yelling over the phone at him. The deputy secured the phone from the dad and advised him that yelling would not help the situation. The deputy radioed the son's telephone number to me.

I called the number, and the subject answered right away. I told him I was Sergeant Sands and I was there to help him. We talked for a while, then he mentioned that I should tell the deputy who was three trailers to the south to duck down. He was an easy target for him to shoot.

I immediately told the deputy to seek better cover.

I talked to the man about it being Easter Sunday. My family was going to have a big dinner tonight. I did not want anything to happen to him that might ruin my day. He seemed to calm down and conversed calmly with me.

Then his sister showed up and asked to talk to her brother. Since he had calmed down, I handed her my phone. She started arguing with him. As I was taking the phone back, the subject fired a round inside the trailer. I immediately checked with the deputy to the south. He was fine!

I talked into the open phoneline to check the man's status. He began talking. He wanted to see how loud the gun would be if he fired it. He had shot the kitchen floor.

We talked for several more minutes about Easter Sunday. He was apologetic about creating such a fuss. He was calm and sounded really tired. I told him if he was ready, he was to leave the gun in the trailer, open the door, and walk out with his hands up.

Within a few minutes, the trailer door opened up. He walked out without the gun and his hands up. One of the deputies put him in handcuffs, and the other secured the gun. He was taken to the hospital psych ward. Just another day at work? I don't think so. This was Easter Sunday. Any coincidence? Jesus works on holidays too!

Chapter 9

Want to Buy LSD on Your Way to High School?

It was about 8:15 in the morning. Students were walking to school. I was in my squad car in a small town. I was about two blocks west of the high school. I could see a large group of students around a car about a block away.

As they saw me, all of the kids on the street began to run toward the school. The car took off rather quickly, but he pulled right over when he saw my red lights go on. As I walked up to the car, he had his hand down between his legs. He was obviously holding and hiding something. I told him to slowly give me what was in his hand.

He handed me a pill bottle about three quarters full, containing white pills. He also had a piece of paper with names on it with a dollar amount next to each name. If the student did not have any cash, he would write their name down and how much they owed.

A city police car drove up. We took the young man down to the local police station and had his car towed after searching it for more contraband.

We advised him of his rights, and he began to be cooperative. He admitted the pills were LSD and he was selling them for $2.00 a hit. We stopped the interview at that point, and I called the high school. I talked to the superintendent of the school district. I advised him what happened and that there were probably students in his school in possession of LSD.

We had a rather lengthy discussion about the danger of the drug. He was going to call an assembly and talk to the students. He was reluctant about sending home a note with each student about what happened. He said it was bad for the school's reputation. Obviously, I disagreed with him.

I transported the offender in my squad car to the jail and turned him over to the detective division for interrogation. I also gave the pill bottle to the detectives for testing.

The detectives arranged for the subject to make a buy from his supplier in the suburbs. I went with them. We met with local detectives who placed a wire on the subject. We took him to his dealer's house. The wire was working fine until someone answered the door. Then the transmission went scratchy and quit. About twenty minutes later the subject returned to our location.

After letting out a few expletives, he was taken back to their police department. I often wonder what happened to him. Hopefully several students were deterred from a life of drugs that day. At one time I believed that my being there on that street that day was pure luck, but now I know it wasn't just luck. I was guided!

Chapter 10

I Fought the Law, and the Law Won!

Now here is another feel-good story about being a police officer! One quiet Saturday night at about 10 P.M., I was patrolling a small town in the northern part of our county. I stopped to confer with the town's parttime police officer, who advised me that even though the local tavern was crowded wall to wall with a popular local band playing, everyone was behaving just fine. Then, as expected, dispatch gave us a call to respond to the tavern. There was a major fight going on inside.

The local officer was relatively new to policework. He said, "I will follow your lead." I told him if we had to end up breaking up a fight or arresting somebody, I had learned to first handcuff the biggest guy fighting. The officer said, "What did you just say?!"

I said, "Look at me. I am six-four, 250 pounds of intimidation. As I was growing up, I was always cautioned by my parents, 'Be careful not to hurt anybody, because you are a big guy.' Every big guy is told that growing up. It is the scrappy little guy that always fights dirty, and he will hurt you way before the big guy does. Take the big guy first, and everyone else will be impressed. The people fighting will stop to watch, and the big guy will comply."

So sure enough, we got inside the tavern, and there was a fight going on, on the dance floor in front of the band. Just like there usually always was, there was a big guy down on the floor, with two to three other guys wailing on him. Tables and chairs were strewn all about.

We walked over to the big guy and told him he was under arrest for disturbing the peace, and we handcuffed him.

We asked him to get up and walk out like a man, but he said he was too hurt and drunk to walk. I told the officer to grab under one armpit and I'd grab the other. We would drag him across the floor to the door and outside. We pushed tables and chairs out of our way and proceeded to drag him.

All of a sudden, the band started playing "I Fought the Law, and the Law Won." The crowd cheered and sang along as we took him outside. What a sendoff!

The fighting was over. No one was hurt in the fight, and the bar owner did not want to press charges. We asked the big guy if there was someone, we could call to take him home. We waited with him until his ride showed up. He was physically fine and even laughed about his sendoff song!

Police work is what you make of it: sometimes very dangerous, sometimes very challenging, and sometimes very fun and rewarding. This one brought smiles on heaven and earth!

Chapter 11

Hitchhiker from Outer Space

As I was driving down the road just west of my town, I noticed a ragged-looking hitchhiker. I stopped and talked to him. He had a meal ID that he said was from a planet that was the third one from the sun. He explained how many light years it took to get there. The laminated card identified his name, his birthday, and the planet that he was from. He was over three hundred years old, by his birthday. He said the ID was good for a meal at any military station.

He was very convincing and serious. I was getting a real education on outer space. He was talking in words that I neither understood nor could re-pronounce. I told him we did not have any military stations nearby, but I would take him to a nearby homeless shelter for the night.

After patting him down again, I put him in my backseat and drove him to the shelter. How many people get to meet a real alien hitchhiker from outer space? Just thought I would throw this true story in as a bonus!

CHAPTER 12

DRIVING WHILE WHAT?!

I was doing stationary patrol, sitting in a utility parking area. That's police language for "waiting for the shift to end." I got a call from dispatch about a possible drunk driver.

A caller had said a car was driving very slowly, weaving from side to side. He also had his dome light on. The location was on the very road I was parked at. Now what's the odds on that?

I could see the car coming from the west, and as it went by my location I could see the dome light was still on. He was driving only 10–15 mph. I immediately pulled in behind him and turned my red lights on. He pulled right over and rolled down his window. He said, "Can I help you, Officer?"

I asked him if he had been drinking tonight. He answered, "No, I was just on my way home from Bible study." I asked him why he had his dome light on. He said they had a very interesting and special meeting that night. He was wanting to learn more!

I told him to set the Bible aside until he got home. He should drive safely home. He responded, "Yes, sir." Looking back at this story, I bet they were smiling above me! Here I was out in the middle of nowhere, closest major road miles away, and at the exact time someone drives by reading a Bible with his dome light on. I remember thinking at the time, "Now that is certainly sending me a message. Hey, don't slack off at the end of your shift."

Chapter 13

Pumpkins on Halloween

It was Halloween Day and I was getting ready to start my shift at 3 P.M. Dispatch called my house. They asked if I could handle a call involving the local skydiving airport. Dispatch advised that a lady came home after work and found a hole in her kitchen ceiling. Upon arrival I met with her. She was very, very upset.

Not only was there a hole in her ceiling, but there were also pumpkin seeds all over the floor and kitchen table. Part of the kitchen table and a chair where she said her daughter sat were broken. She was crying as she spoke.

Looking up through the hole in the kitchen ceiling, I could see a hole in the roof. There were parts of shingles also on the floor. Her kitchen looked like a tornado had ripped through it.

She said she had called the skydiving office, about 1.5 miles away. The office admitted that there were three skydivers that had taken a pumpkin skydiving with them. It was Halloween! They had lost control of the pumpkin and did not know where it landed.

The complainant wanted the three guys arrested! No ifs, ands, or buts! Put them in jail and throw away the key! Soon the south zone deputy arrived. We went over to the skydiving office where the three guys were waiting for us. They were very apologetic. They offered to cover all repair costs and to give the owners a heartfelt apology.

Their story was that because it was Halloween, they brought a carved pumpkin to pass back and forth as they dove. After the first man jumped, he lost control of the pumpkin.

I recontacted the owner of the house. She was still extremely upset and wanted the three arrested. I told them they were under arrest and they would be booked at our jail. They willingly went with us.

The following morning, I got a call from dispatch. CBS National News had heard of the event and wanted to do a story for the CBS Evening News. I volunteered the deputy that was with me the previous night to do the interview. Sure enough, it was the lead story on Dan Rather CBS national news! We made the big time!

The skydivers pleaded not guilty at the trial. The three men were scientists who worked at a nearby research facility. During the trial they offered to pay restitution. They did not challenge any of the victim's or officers' testimonies. When it was the defense's turn, one of the scientists took the stand. He had several papers and charts with him.

He got into a lengthy testimony about if the wind had been two miles an hour stronger or two degrees more to the south, where the pumpkin might have landed. The judge had enough of the irrelevant testimony. He cut off the witness. The trial was over! They were convicted of reckless conduct and fined and ordered to pay complete restitution. The three scientists looked stunned.

We slapped each other on the back about the judge's reaction! As we walked outside, I distinctly remember the sun coming out from behind a cloud. Even heaven was happy with that decision! Happy Halloween!

Chapter 14

A Girdle Story

Now some of you might not remember what a girdle was. It was a tight band worn by women around their stomachs to help them look thinner. Here is a funny story that turned tragic. It is not a story I am proud of, but it did happen.

Before I joined the sheriff's department, I worked three years at a university police department. We operated both squad cars and a station wagon with red lights and a stretcher in it. The station wagon operated as a police vehicle and an ambo-wagon.

One night on patrol we got a call at the university center about a lady having trouble breathing. We arrived in a few minutes and were directed to the ballroom, where a conference was taking place. We found the lady. She was sitting upright in a chair, having trouble breathing. At the time we did not carry oxygen with us.

We got her to stand and onto the stretcher. As she tried to lie down, she could not breathe. So, we put her back in the chair. We rolled the chair and her down the hallway. We got her to a squad car and in the back seat. I had a young rookie officer with me. I had him sit in the back with the lady to monitor her wellbeing. We took off enroute to the hospital with red lights and siren.

After just a few moments, the lady began to loudly complain that she could not breathe. She said her girdle was too tight, causing her the breathing problems. Now my partner was barely twenty-one years old. He had no idea what a girdle was! Looking in the rearview mirror, I could see the lady trying to lift her skirt up and dislodge the girdle. My partner was turning white and was completely flabbergasted.

He tried his best to assist her. We were now going at a faster speed. When we got to the emergency room, we were met by hospital staff. They immediately put oxygen on her and took her into the hospital.

On the way back I teased the young officer about what had happened in the back seat. It was coming up on shift change. I couldn't wait to tell the two shifts about the story and tease my partner in good fun!

Then as we were all laughing in the squad room, the phone rang. The lady had just died of a massive heart attack caused by the breathing problem. It was so quiet you could have heard an ant crawling across the floor. We were all saying silent prayers for the lady. It was so stunning that I am sure everyone in that room still remembers that day. No one moved for several minutes, until we all silently left the squad room, some going home, some beginning their shifts.

What a lesson for all of us, especially me! Life and death can change so quickly in our line of work.

Chapter 15

Bone Sticking Out! Hot Coffee!

One winter when I was working for the university police, we got a call to the lagoon on campus where people ice skated. A male had been injured ice skating. Upon arrival we could hear him screaming from the parking lot. We ran out on the ice to see something I will never forget. The man had a broken leg. One of his two lower leg bones was sticking out of his leg and pants. There was blood everywhere! We immediately called for the city to send an ambulance for transport. It seemed like forever for them to get there, but I am sure it was just a matter of minutes.

Another incident on campus involved a man who had spilled a full pot of hot coffee on his lap. As we approached the building he was in, we could hear his screams of agony. We tended to him with cool towels. As he began to cool down, the pain began to lessen. He was a very strong man, and he was able to get control of his emotions. We got him to the emergency room as soon as possible. That sound of his agony still haunts me today.

Both incidents taught me that no matter what is going on around you, you as a police officer have a duty and responsibility to remain calm, cool, and collected. If you don't, you do not deserve to wear the badge. Use each experience as a learning tool. Trust in your own abilities but believe you cannot do it all alone. Have help on your shoulder, and *he* will get you through.

CHAPTER 16

ARMED ROBBER WARRANT STOP-AND-SHOP

One of the jobs I liked doing at the sheriff's department was working on the warrant list. I would track people down, and sometimes it got very exciting. One week a new warrant came out for an armed robber of a local Stop-and-Shop convenience store. We did not have a good address to check, but I had an address for his mother.

I went and talked with her. She did not know where he was staying, but she had a house phone number for him in the university area. I called the local phone company. They advised that they could not give out addresses of a phone number. I readvised her who I was, my job title, and the telephone number to the sheriff's department. She reluctantly gave me her first name only.

Then it got to be fun—a test of wills. I asked for her supervisor. She would only give me a first name of the supervisor. She said her supervisor would get back to me next week. Now, I am usually a very pleasant person. I don't like to argue. But to me, this was a dangerous public situation.

We knew the robber was still in the area. He still had a gun. He could conduct another robbery at any time. He was a danger to the public. His mother even wanted him arrested before he did something else stupid and somebody got shot! He could kill somebody or a police officer.

Finally, I wore down the telephone operator. I told her if somebody got hurt, she and her supervisor could be indicted for withholding information. And of course, they would be personally sued civilly. I would gladly testify against them. The supervisor must have been listening to our conversation. Suddenly the supervisor was on the phone. She said she would give me the address this time only. Of course, I politely said okay and thanked her.

I went to the address the supervisor gave me. I asked for a backup car from the city. We went and knocked on the door. A young man answered the door. We asked if the warrant subject was there. The young man did not reply right away. We told him we had an arrest warrant for the subject. He never did answer us, but he rolled his eyes in an upward motion, indicating the subject was upstairs.

We told him we had probable cause to search the house. We then went up the stairs carefully. In searching the bedrooms, we checked each closet. In the second bedroom, we noticed a pile of dirty clothes on the closet floor. We instinctively knew he was under the clothes. With guns drawn, we ordered him to come out. As the clothes moved, he came out with his hands up.

No gun was on him. We asked where it was, and he glanced quickly at the bed. We found the gun under the bed. He was handcuffed, and I took him to jail.

Something told me to call the telephone operator back. I really didn't want to. But I reluctantly did with a smile on my face. I wanted to ensure her she did the right thing in giving us the address. She was helping to protect the public from another incident. Sometimes officers have to convince people it is their duty to help.

Man, I like this job! Being a police officer can be fun.

CHAPTER 17

MURDER WARRANT FROM PENNSYLVANIA

Our police dispatch center told me to call them by telephone about a wanted subject on our warrant list. They did not want to broadcast the info to members of the general public who might have a police scanner. Dispatch advised that they had been contacted by a Pennsylvania police department. That department had a current address in our county where a man wanted for murder was staying. He was wanted for murdering his wife.

I asked if we had a detective on duty. We did, so he responded to the location. The plan was to have the plain clothes detective and me go to the door and calmly advise them we had a message for the wanted man. A detective in plain clothes and a sergeant were far less intimidating than several officers with guns drawn. We had a couple of city officers respond for backup also.

We knocked on the apartment door and asked if he was there. He came walking up to the door, and we asked him to step outside, which he did. We told him we had a warrant for his arrest for murdering his wife. He insisted that could not be—his wife was in the apartment.

We said not her but his previous wife. After we got him handcuffed, we talked to the new wife and advised her what was happening. She did not even know he was previously married.

Now we could have handled this a variety of different ways, due to the severity of the crime. But our calmness and an element of surprise worked a lot better than kicking the door in and grabbing the subject.

How to answer police calls comes with police experience. Call it a gut feeling, call it intuition or, as I believe now, I had help on my shoulder.

Chapter 18

The Big Bang

On a nice quiet evening, I had the toughest call that one can imagine. As you will read, this call was not made for everyone to handle. How would you have handled it, after reading the above stories? You will see similarities.

Dispatch advised that I should go to the local hospital. The zone car was on another call. A patient had dropped off a suspicious package that they believed would explode. The patient was still there.

Upon arrival I met with an excited hospital custodian who was pointing at a bottle on the floor. He said he was told it was a bomb. To make matters worse, it was placed right in front of a large blue arrow painted on the wall that said "Oxygen."

A man whom I knew as the director of the local homeless shelter came walking up. He told me that one of his guests at the shelter had been acting exceptionally weird. He kept talking about blowing himself up. The director had talked him into going to the hospital so he could talk to a counselor.

On the way to the hospital, the man told the director he built bombs. He even had one go off in his second-floor apartment, breaking a few windows. He said the police were called. The director asked him if he had a bomb on him right then. To the director's surprise, the man pulled out a bottle with a wick on it as they pulled into the ER parking lot. They walked to the ER entrance, and the subject gave the bottle to the director.

They entered the ER and the director put the bottle down on the floor next to, of all places!, a large blue painted arrow that said "Oxygen".

As I walked down to the subject's room, I had dispatch call the city police to see if they had a record on the subject. They had already pulled the report of his blowing out his apartment windows.

I interviewed the subject. I asked him exactly what was in the bottle and how it went off. He said that the ingredients were alcohol, granulated ammonia, two AA batteries, and a cloth wick in a glass beer bottle.

He said the two AA batteries heat up when placed in a mixture of alcohol and granulated ammonia. The ingredients reached a temperature at which there is a flash/bang explosion!

I asked him how long it takes, and he said from a few minutes to a couple of hours, depending on the chemical reaction. He admitted he had one go off in his apartment, blowing out his windows.

The sheriff's department did not have a bomb squad. I called the nearest department that did. They were 45-60 minutes away! I explained the situation and asked them what I could do.

The bomb squad leader advised that the ER and nearby parts of the hospital should be immediately evacuated. They were familiar with these types of explosives. This was a real threat!

The fact that it was next to the oxygen arrow really upset him. He advised that we could lose a good part of the hospital if it went off because the pure oxygen would magnify the explosion!

I talked to the ER doctor in charge. He explained that it was a busy Saturday night—all beds were full and he was not evacuating. Now what?! Should I force an evacuation? That didn't seem probable. Should I just wait 45–60 minutes for the bomb squad? That was also a bad option.

The excited custodian was standing next to me. I looked down at the bottle. I told the custodian to open the doors. I was taking the bomb outside. He loudly shouted, "No!"

By that time, I had the bottle in my hand and was going out the door. I took it out about one hundred yards and placed it next to a fencepost. I ran back to the hospital. The janitor hugged me and said, "You are my hero!" Little did I know at the time, but the hero was on my shoulder!

The bomb squad arrived on time. They had been advised that the bomb was no longer in the ER. They arrived driving what looked like a cement mixer, a large round cylinder on a truck bed.

The bomb squad technician put on a bombproof suit that looked like he was going to land on the moon. He walked out and picked up the bottle. He placed it in the cement cylinder. We went to a nearby gravel pit. At a safe range, we shot the bottle and it went flash/bang.

Of course, the episode made the next-day newspaper headlines.

Would you have carried the bomb out? Remember, I had that calm sensation of no fear. *Why?* He was on my shoulder!

CHAPTER 19

COMPLETED SUICIDES

One of the worst kinds of police calls is a successful suicide. I handled several suicides over the years, but two I will never forget. I got a call of a suicide in one of our northern towns. Upon arrival, I was met by witnesses who described the following: A man had been drinking heavily on his birthday. He was deeply depressed. He left his friends and walked to the nearby railroad crossing.

He walked eastbound on the tracks from the intersection. He sat down facing west. An eastbound freight train was bearing down on his location. The train could not stop in time. The man was literally thrown off the track in pieces. We spent several hours cleaning up the scene. On my own birthday I always remember that guy.

I investigated another suicide on Christmas Eve. I was driving into a south county forest preserve, not too far from my house. I noticed a car by one of the shelters. Its engine was running. As I shined the spotlight on the vehicle, I could see a hose going from the car's tailpipe into the passenger-side window. All of the windows were fogged up.

I advised dispatch about a possible suicide in progress. I asked for the local fire department to respond. I went up to the vehicle and opened the driver's door. The man was obviously deceased. Soon the fire department arrived. The man was from out of the area. Now on every Christmas Eve, I think of that man.

The moral to these stories is that sometimes we as police officers have the unthinkable thrown at us. Holidays and birthdays sometimes have a different meaning to us. Thank goodness we have that helper on our shoulder to calm our nerves and make it possible to help others!

Chapter 20

Nice to Have the Boss on Your Side!

One thing that makes a police officer better is the boss. I was lucky to have two of the finest sheriffs. They ran tough, tight ships, but they also stood up for their officers. Here is my finest moment of support.

Now this story is several years old, when cannabis was illegal. My supervisor and I were riding together in my squad car one night. We were following a car northbound on a blacktop from one of our small towns. There was a painted centerline down the road.

We noticed the dome light in the car come on. Then we saw the passenger lighting a cigarette. He passed it to the driver to take a drag. Then the driver passed it back to the passenger. They did this several times. The driver was swerving back and forth across the centerline.

I activated my red lights and stopped him to check his sobriety. He pulled over right away. As I walked up to his car, he rolled down his window. My supervisor was shining his spotlight in the back seat.

I could smell a very strong odor, which I recognized as cannabis. I told the driver that he needed to exit the vehicle. My supervisor had the man on his side of the car also exit. We searched the car and the subjects and found more cannabis. My supervisor asked the driver for the car keys; we were going to search the trunk also.

The driver handed him a set of keys. None of the keys opened the trunk. My supervisor strongly suggested to him to give us the right set of keys. He gave us a second set, which worked fine to open the trunk.

To our surprise the trunk was full of brown paper bags full of packaged cannabis. We obviously had stopped a dealer on his delivery run. We told both subjects they were under arrest for possession of and intent to deliver cannabis. We towed their vehicle and transported them to the jail and turned them over to our detectives.

Of course, they pleaded not guilty. When the trial came up, we both testified to the above facts. Their defense lawyer asked to approach the bench. He said the officers did not have probable cause to stop and search the vehicle. The defendant's rights had been violated. The case should be thrown out.

The state's attorney started to present our probable cause when the judge said, "Case dismissed." We were all dumbfounded. The SA was furious! The judge said sternly, "Next case."

We walked out of the courthouse and directly over to the sheriff's office. The sheriff had already been advised we were coming to see him. He was a bright red color. He was very mad and upset. We had never seen him like that; we had only heard stories. We barely began telling him what happened when he said, "I have heard enough! Nobody, but *nobody*, treats my deputies that way!"

He bolted past us directly enroute to the judge's chambers. In the courthouse, they said everyone on the first floor could hear the sheriff yelling from the third floor at the judge! We heard rumors weeks later. One of the guys we arrested had a father that had personal ties with the judge! There were no consequences for anyone—case dismissed. We went back to work.

Now those were the good old days! When a cop was a cop and a sheriff could be a sheriff. Having the sheriff back you up and stick his head on the chopping block probably is not seen in today's society. Even though we lost this case to a crooked system, we continued to do our jobs because we knew we had backup, both within the department and in our personal lives' pursuit of helping the public. That calmness of knowing what is right and what is wrong allowed me to cope. I wish I had realized earlier the calling that I had.

Chapter 21

What Do You Want to Do Next?

In this last story, you get to put yourself in the scenario. There will be a point when I ask you, "What would you do next?" I bet it will not be what I chose to do!

I was the training officer for a new young recruit. We were patrolling the northern part of the county. We got a call that was one for the books. Put your thinking hat on as I describe the scenario.

The call was from the husband. He was afraid his wife had hurt herself. She had locked herself in their bedroom following a domestic argument. He had knocked on the door several times and yelled to her several times with no response. I asked that the local fire department be put on standby.

I had a queasy feeling about this call. This was not going to be your ordinary family dispute. I was going to need some more help. I felt that calmness and confidence coming over me. I was not alone!

We conferred with the husband in his kitchen. He showed us the bedroom with the locked door, which he had been pounding on for several minutes. He had banged so hard that he had put a hole in the hollow door. I knocked on the door several times, stating I was the police and assuring that I was there to help her. I asked, "What can I do for you?" I got no response at all.

The husband explained that he did have a gun in a case inside the bedroom. He was afraid she might use it on herself or anyone else entering the room. They had been having marital issues for a while, and things had been very intense.

My supervisor called a status check on us, saying he was nearby if we needed him. I asked him to respond as soon as possible. He arrived within a few minutes, and we filled him in on the dilemma. His response was "What do *you* want to do next?" He knew from previous incidents that I had the situation analyzed and a plan formed. He had complete confidence in me and maybe he knew I was getting divine help.

I asked the husband if he had a tire iron in his garage. I wanted to make the hole in the door bigger so I could see more of the room. He got the tire iron, and I made a larger hole. I could now see their bed. On the far side of the bed away from the door, I could see the top few inches of the back of her head. She seemed to be sitting on the floor.

I continually called out her name, but she never responded. I made the hole bigger yet, and now I could see an open pistol box with no gun in it. The rookie deputy turned to me then and asked, "What are *you* going to do next?"

I said I was going to stick my hand through the hole in the door and grab the inside handle and open the door. I remember six bulging eyes looking at me! I opened the door and there was no response from the wife. The husband said, "What are *you* going to do next?"

Now I was really scratching my head! I told them I was going to enter the room and walk around the end of the bed until I could see her. Was she still alive? Was she hurt? Did she have the gun? As I approached, she did not move at all. Yes, she was still breathing. Her eyes were wide open staring out a nearby window. She had the gun on her lap. The gun was cocked, and her finger was on the trigger!

At that point, I backed up out of the room. She remained motionless. All three of the men said in unison, "What are *you* going to do next?"

Okay, your turn! What would you, the reader, do next? I wish there were a way I could hear your answers!

This is where and when I had internal help of just knowing what to do. It was as though someone was in my head telling me the plan. What would work? What were we going to do?

After a pause, I said, "Here is the plan," I laid it out and everyone knew exactly what to do and when to do it. There was really no discussion of alternatives.

"I am going to walk back in there. As I go around the end of the bed, I am going to take two large steps toward her. On the third step, I am going to forcibly step downward on the gun. If it goes off, it will only hurt her leg! When you see me going for the third step, I want you two guys (the supervisor and the deputy) to grab her by the shoulders and pull her up on the bed. To work, this has to happen all at the same time. When I take that third step, you grab her!"

It worked to perfection. The gun did not go off. The wife was now successfully lying on the bed. She was moving her eyes, looking at us, but she did not speak. She had that look of *What in the hell just happened?!* It was over in a matter of seconds.

We radioed the fire rescue, who was in the driveway. We told them it was safe to come in, and they transported her to the hospital.

Now that is a real police rescue call! Do you think I had external help? I now believe I did!

Conclusion

I hoped you enjoyed my story, how I was able to handle these situations with help on my shoulder. Expect the unexpected and be able to adapt! I hope you found them entertaining, constructive, and inspirational.

When I did the job of a police officer for twenty-five years, I had no doubts about public support. We were welcomed wherever we went. There was no undermining our status. But at the same time, we were expected to handle the situation with professionalism. Whatever happened, we had the job of making the right decisions. Some of that comes with training, some comes from experience, and some comes from intuition.

Yet there is more. What do you do when it isn't covered in training, experience, or intuition? You may have to make life-and-death decisions. You have to reach into your inner strengths. I would rapidly access what I needed to do and what I needed not to do. Perhaps the second part of that sentence is more important. This is where I realized I was not alone.

We all experience close calls in life. What caused us to make the right decision? Example: taking a second look for oncoming traffic. Is it just luck? Is it just coincidence? Or is there more?

I travelled through my career with self-confidence and a feeling that I could handle whatever was thrown at me. Why? Looking back, it has become obvious. I had a helper on my shoulder. Jesus would guide me without my knowing I was being guided.

If you think about your life and the decisions you have made, I'll bet the farm that you also had help on your shoulder.

Thank you for reading my story!

Sergeant Dennis R. Sands
DeKalb County Sheriff's Department

www.ingramcontent.com/pod-product-compliance
Lightning Source LLC
LaVergne TN
LVHW051130210926
848482LV00001B/46
9798891276949